THE STORY BEHIND
MOTORCYCLE RACING

WRITTEN BY PAUL ROBINSON

CONTENTS

INTRODUCTION TO MOTORCYCLE RACING	4	MOTOCROSS	10
RED HOT RACERS	6	FREESTYLE JUMPS	12
MOTORCYCLE RACING GEAR	8	MOTOGP	14
		RACE THE WORLD	16

DISCLAIMER:
The activities in this book have been performed by people who are experienced professionals, or by people who have had professional training. Neither the publisher nor the author shall be liable for any bodily harm or damage to property whatsoever that may be caused or sustained as a result of conducting any of the activities featured in this book.

Words in **BOLD** can be found in the glossary.

SUPERBIKES	18	THE HALL OF FAME	26
SPEEDWAY	20	RECORD BREAKERS	28
IT TAKES TWO	22	GLOSSARY	30
FACE THE FEAR	24	INDEX	31

INTRODUCTION TO MOTORCYCLE RACING

Motorcycle racing is fast, competitive, and exciting! There are many different types of races for fans to enjoy. The bikes, rules, and tracks may be different for each event, but all riders have a fierce desire to win!

EARLY DAYS

In 1868, American Sylvester Roper made an early type of motorcycle driven by steam that he claimed could "outrun any horse". The first motorcycle driven by petrol was invented in Germany in 1885. It was made of wood and had a top speed of 7 miles per hour (11 km/h).

HOW THEY WORK

Motorcycles are powered by a piston inside a cylinder. Fuel is burnt to drive the piston up and down. The piston turns a shaft, which goes to the gearbox. The gearbox drives a chain that turns the bike's rear wheel. The cylinder is measured in **cc**: the bigger the cylinder, the more powerful the bike.

DID YOU KNOW?

The first known motorcycle race was held in 1894. The race was in France, and went from Paris to Rouen, a distance of almost 80 miles (126 km/h). The winner had an average speed of 10 miles per hour (16 km/h).

TYPES OF MOTORCYCLE RACING

There are many different types of motorcycle racing!

MOTOCROSS

MOTOGP

SUPERBIKES

FREESTYLE

SPEEDWAY

RED HOT RACERS

Motorcycle racing takes many forms, but top riders share one thing: the skill they show in the heat of a race! Skill doesn't come easily, it can take many hours of training and practice.

AROUND THE WORLD

Today, motorcycle racing is an international sport, with racers from all over the world taking part in high-speed races. Modern bikes can easily be pushed faster than 200 miles per hour (320 km/h).

DID YOU KNOW?
Some racing bikes are **modified** versions of bikes that are available for anyone to buy!

DOING IT RIGHT

Crashes and even death are part of motorcycle racing. The best riders understand that control is as important as speed. They are competitive but follow the rules to reduce injuries from accidents. **Sponsors** expect their riders to follow high standards and win fairly.

BEING FAIR

All motorcycle racing around the world is watched over by the FIM – Fédération Internationale de Motocyclisme. They set rules so that events are safe and fair.

MOTORCYCLE RACING GEAR

Riders wear similar safety gear across all the different motor sports. The rules state that safety gear has to be worn in practice and during every race, to protect the riders from the dangers of racing.

HELMET
A crash helmet is essential as it protects riders from head injuries. Most helmets have built-in tinted visors, but in some sports, riders wear a separate pair of goggles to protect their eyes.

BACK PROTECTORS
Back protectors are often sewn into an undersuit. They are flexible so the rider can still move easily, but strong enough to reduce the impact of a crash and protect the rider from spinal injuries.

BOOTS

Racing boots cover the foot and ankle and are fastened tightly so they don't come off in a crash. They are padded everywhere except the soles, which are thin so riders can feel how the bike is performing.

KNEE PADS

Some racing suits, like in MotoGP, have sliders on the outside of the rider's knees. They wear down as they drag on the track (when the rider leans into a corner), but are easily replaced.

RACING SUIT AND GLOVES

Riders' suits and gloves are made of leather, because it's thick, hard to rip, and gives good grip on the bike. They are often specially made for each rider to make sure they fit perfectly.

MOTOCROSS

Motocross is also known as MX or dirt bike racing. Riders race on a cross-country track of mud or sand, that can be between 1 and 3 miles (1.5 and 5 km) long. MX bikes are light to help riders twist around tight bends and jump over hills on the track.

WORLD CHAMPIONSHIPS

The FIM Motocross World Championship is run over more than 20 events at exciting locations around the world. Riders compete to gather points across two 30-minute races at each location. The rider with the most points wins the trophy!

SUPERCROSS

Supercross is a newer sport. It's raced inside a stadium on shorter tracks which have sharper, sudden corners that put riders' reflexes to the test. They also have really steep jumps – riders can soar 10.5 metres (35 ft) in the air during a race. It's not for the fainthearted!

TRUE STORY

Children as young as 6 can learn to ride and compete in mini-bike races. Top rider John Hopkins started as a child. By 18, he was competing against adults and winning championships!

DID YOU KNOW?

Motocross bikes are designed to cope with complex tracks: they have **shock absorbers** for landing smoothly after a jump, thick tyres for gripping onto the loose track, and engines with powerful **acceleration**.

FREESTYLE JUMPS

Freestyle motocross – also known as FMX – is a thrilling variation of motocross. The riders pull off stunts and jumps to impress judges and gain points. There are two types of freestyle events, these are big air and freestyle motocross.

DID YOU KNOW?
Riders use foam pits or giant air bags to try out new mid-air stunts. This gives them a safe landing area – if the trick goes wrong, the rider and bike have a soft place to land.

TIME TO SHINE

In big air events, riders get two jumps, usually covering a distance of 23 metres (75 ft) from a dirt-covered ramp to perform a stunt. In freestyle events, they perform two stunt routines, which can include multiple jumps and stunts, across a larger area. Routines last about 15 minutes.

SHOWING OFF

The best freestyle riders can do really complex, impressive flips and tricks in mid-air. Here's some of the most daring.

SEAT GRAB HEART ATTACK

SUPERMAN BACKFLIP

LAZY BOY

TRUE STORY

In 2012, American motorcyclist Alex Harvill broke the world record for the longest motorcycle jump from a ramp. He covered 130 metres (425 ft) – that's longer than a football pitch!

MOTOGP

MotoGP is short for "Motorcycle Grand Prix". Races are held all over the world. Riders and their teams travel to take part in these events and win points. The season runs for about nine months. The rider with the most points at the end becomes World Champion.

MOVING ON

With flat racetracks and wide corners, MotoGP is the best place to compete for speed. In the first championship in 1949, the fastest bike reached a top speed of 140 miles per hour (225 km/h). Today, modern MotoGP bikes are able to reach speeds of 225 miles per hour (362 km/h)!

LICENCE TO SPEED

In MotoGP, riders want to maintain their fast speeds, even when going round corners! To do this, they lean into the bend, with their knee or elbow dragging on the ground. This balances the bike and keeps them fast!

DID YOU KNOW?

MotoGP racers push their bikes to the limit, driving them so hard and fast that the engines need stripping and rebuilding after racing. Teams are restricted in the number of engines they can use in a season.

TRUE STORY

Giacomo Agostini is one of the best MotoGP drivers in history. He won a total of 15 world championship titles during his career! It will be hard for anyone to beat this record.

15

RACE THE WORLD

In MotoGP, you can work your way up to the bigger and faster classes of the championship. On race weekends, 3 classes start: Moto 2; Moto 3; and MotoGP. These bikes range from speeds of 150 to 220 miles per hour (240 to 355 km/h)!

TOP TEAMS

MotoGP isn't just about the riders – lots of people work behind the scenes to help riders perform their best, break records, and win races. From the factory team who build the bike, to the mechanics who make sure it's able to run at top speed, MotoGP is a team effort.

WINNING TECHNIQUE

A good rider reaches top speed on the track's **straights**, and brakes hard into the corners. Winning takes courage and control – in close races, bikes are just inches apart! Top riders see the bike ahead as a challenge, not a sign of defeat.

DID YOU KNOW?

MotoGP riders are very fit – controlling the heavy bike while flying around the track at high speed is hard work. To avoid becoming dehydrated, riders have special helmets that they can drink water from!

TRUE STORY

In one legendary race during the 2016 Italian MotoGP, the top 5 riders finished within 0.077 seconds of each other! That's a close finish.

SUPERBIKES

Superbikes have 1,000cc engines and are truly fast! They are ordinary road bikes that have been specifically modified for the race. That means superbike fans can buy motorcycles that look like the ones on the track but, of course, they won't go as fast!

SUPERBIKE WORLD

The first World Superbike Championship was in 1988. At that time, superbikes were much more powerful than MotoGP bikes. The gap in power and speed has closed in recent years and some MotoGP bikes are now faster than superbikes!

SPOT THE DIFFERENCE

Teams modify superbikes to improve their performance, but most racing rules require the bike to have the same overall look as its road-going version. Modifications usually include adding power to the engine, making the bike lighter, and giving it a more efficient **exhaust**.

DID YOU KNOW?

Some Superbike and MotoGP races take place on the same circuits around the world. Others are unique to each type of racing. In the UK, the Superbike World Championship is hosted at Donnington Park, and MotoGP takes place at Silverstone.

Casey Stoner at Silverstone, UK

TRUE STORY

In 2004, James Toseland became the youngest ever World Superbike champion. He was 24 years old.

SPEEDWAY

Speedway bikes have amazing power. With 500-cc engines and running on **methanol fuel**, they can accelerate to reach 60 miles per hour (97 km/h) faster than a **Formula 1** car! Riders have to be brave – these bikes have no brakes!

SPEEDWAY MEETS

Each country has multiple leagues. Teams in each league compete against each other in rounds of races called "heats". With every heat, weaker teams get knocked out until one winner remains! These are called league championships, but there are also world championships.

BARE BONES

Speedway racing is not for the fainthearted. To turn corners, the rider slides the back wheel sideways. Because there are no brakes, it is easy to make a mistake. Riders frequently hit the walls, the gravel track, and other bikes!

Inner track edge

DID YOU KNOW?

Riders are knocked out of the heat if both wheels of their bike cross the inner or outer edge of the track! The only exception is if they were forced to do this to stay safe.

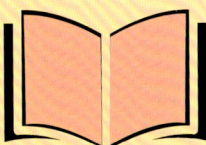

TRUE STORY

Australian motorcycle racer Jason Crump finished in second place in the 2001, 2002, and 2003 Speedway World Championships. In 2004, he finally succeeded in winning the title. He won 3 times in his career.

IT TAKES TWO

The most unusual-looking motorcycle racing is sidecar racing. Sidecars have three wheels. The motor is positioned under the driver, and the passenger sits on a platform behind one of the rear wheels. These races require the skills of the driver and passenger to control the sidecar at top speeds!

INCHES ABOVE THE TRACK

Sidecar racing became popular in the 1920s, but the first MotoGP sidecar races took place in 1949. It's a thrilling ride for the driver and passenger, sitting just a few centimetres (few inches) above the track and reaching speeds of 160 miles per hour (260 km/h).

SPEED MACHINES

The **aerodynamic** design of a sidecar helps it go fast, but the riders affect speed too. Passengers must lean and move about the platform, transferring their weight from right to left depending on the bend, and forwards and backwards to help keep the wheels on the ground.

TRUE STORY

British rider Steve Webster retired in 2005. He had been racing for over 20 years, winning 10 world sidecar titles. In 2004, Steve won the "triple" – the British, European, and World Championships.

Road-going sidecars look very different from the ones that race!

FACE THE FEAR

Motorcycle racing can never be totally safe, and medical teams are on hand at every event. Riders' mental preparation is as vital as a physical warm-up – they cannot lose concentration for a moment.

WEIGHING UP THE RISKS

Even the most skilled riders are aware of the risks they face every time they go onto the track. Despite all the modern safety precautions, a high-speed fall is still dangerous. But racing is a thrill that most professionals don't want to give up!

ROAD RACERS

The Isle of Man TT (Tourist Trophy) is held on a 38-mile (61-km) loop on public roads on a small island off the coast of Britain. It is one of the most dangerous races for riders. It is also the oldest. It has been held every year since 1907, and thousands of bike fans go to watch.

DID YOU KNOW?

Whle turning a corner, the amount of the MotoGP tyre that is touching the ground is no bigger than a coin!

TRUE STORY

Superbike racer Mike Booth has had many life-changing injuries – in 2022, a crash left him with multiple breaks in his legs, leading to one of his lower legs being amputated. He is already back racing!

THE HALL OF FAME

The top motorcycle riders are heroes to their fans.

VALENTINO ROSSI

Valentino is considered one of the greatest MotoGP riders of all time. He won his first title in Italy in 1994 at the age of 15. He went onto win a total of nine MotoGP World Championships, which makes him one of the most successful motorcycle racers ever. When he retired, his famous number 46 retired with him.

MICK DOOHAN

Arguably the best Australian MotoGP racer ever, Mick won the 500cc World Championship five times in a row from 1994-8. Mick loved taking part in tough races with other top riders. He had to retire after a crash in Spain, but he is still seen as a hero of the track.

KENNY ROBERTS

One name, two generations of American heroes. Kenny Roberts senior had some great races and won the 1978 500cc MotoGP World Championship. Kenny held the title for the next two years. Kenny's son, Kenny junior, then won the same title in 2000.

DID YOU KNOW?

In 2010, Rocky Robinson from the USA, recorded the fastest ever speed on a motorcycle by reaching 377 mph (606 km/h). The motorcycle, which was specially built to be amazingly fast, is called Ack Attack. It looks quite different from regular motorcycles!

RECORD BREAKERS

The history books of motorcycle racing are filled with amazing record breakers. There are so many impressive moments to learn about. These are the things that have changed the way people think about the sport.

MOST SPEEDWAY WORLD CUP WINS

In 2001, Jason Crump won all 10 of the races he competed in in the Speedway World Cup! That's an impressive achievement.

FIRST DOUBLE FRONT FLIP ON MOTORCYCLE

In 2016, Gregg Duffy completed the first ever double front flip on a motorcycle. Not only did this win him a Guinness World Record, it also won him the FMX Best Trick award.

FASTEST SPEED DRAGGED BEHIND A MOTORCYCLE

In 2024, stunt rider Jonny Davies achieved the fastest speed while being dragged behind a motorcycle. He reached 160 miles per hour (257 km/h) while "skiing" behind a modified Kawasaki Ninja H2 SX.

LONGEST MOTORCYCLE RACE CIRCUIT

The 38-mile (61-km) "Mountain" circuit on the Isle of Man is the longest used for any motorcycle race. It also has a total of 264 corners!

WHAT IT TAKES TO BE THE BEST

It takes lots of mental and physical strength, training time, and dedication to break a world record in any motorcycle sport. Depending on the type of record, people don't always break it on their first attempt. Once the record is broken, they also have to hold onto it! This means defending your record if someone else breaks it.

GLOSSARY

Acceleration – the process of speeding up.

Aerodynamic – something that is shaped to travel quickly and easily.

cc – this unit of measurement refers to the size of a vehicle's engine. The bigger the cc, the more powerful the engine.

Exhaust – a pipe at the back of a vehicle, which waste gas and liquid produced by the engine's cylinder escapes from.

Formula 1 (F1) – a huge international racing series for single-seater racing cars which is held annually.

Freestyle – a stunt competition in which the rider can choose the movements that are performed.

Methanol fuel – an explosive type of fuel that can generate lots of power.

Modified – changed. People often modify motorcycles to make them better suited to race conditions. Some races are strict on what modifications are allowed.

Shock absorbers – part of the suspension of a vehicle that helps it drive smoothly.

Sponsors – a company that pays someone to advertise their company. In sports, a sportsperson or athlete may wear clothing or drive a vehicle with the sponsor company's logo on it.

Straights – the fastest sections of motocross tracks. Straights are not long, but they are difficult to ride because the ground is very rough.

Superbike – a fast, powerful bike modified from a model that's on sale to the public.

INDEX

A
Ack Attack (bike) 27
Agostini, Giacomo 15

B
Booth, Mike 25

C
Crump, Jason 21, 28

D
Davies, Jonny 28
Dirt bike racing
 (see: *Motocross*)
Donnington Park, UK 19
Doohan, Mick 26
Duffy, Gregg 28

G
Gear 8-9
Guinness World Record 28

F
FIM (Fédération Internationale de Motocyclisme) 7
FIM Motocross World Champioship 10
Freestyle motocross
 Big air events 12-13
 Freestyle events 5, 12-13
 Tricks and stunts 12-13, 28

H
Harvill, Alex 13
Hopkins, John 11

I
Isle of Man TT 25, 28

K
Kawasaki Ninja H2 SX 28

M
Modifications 6, 18, 28, 30
Motocross 5, 10-11, 12-13
MotoGP 5, 9, 14-15, 16-17, 18-19, 22, 26-27
MX (see: *Motocross*)

R
Roberts, Kenny 27
Robinson, Rocky, 27
Roper, Sylvester 4
Rossi, Valentino 26

S
Sidecar racing 22-23
Silverstone, UK 19
Speedway 5, 20-21, 28
Stoner, Casey 19
Superbikes 5, 18-19, 25, 30
Supercross 11

T
Toseland, James 19
True stories 11, 13, 15, 17, 19, 21, 23, 25

W
Webster, Steve 23
World championships 10-11, 14-15, 16, 18-19, 21, 23, 26-27
World records 13, 15, 16, 19, 27, 28-29

HUNGRY TOMATO

Copyright © 2025 Hungry Tomato Ltd

First published in 2025 by Hungry Tomato Ltd
F15, Old Bakery Studios, Blewetts Wharf,
Malpas Road, Truro, Cornwall,
TR1 1QH, UK.

No part of this publication may be reproduced, stored in a retrieval system, or transmitted in any form or by any means, electronic, mechanical, photocopying, recording, or otherwise, without prior written permission of the copyright owner.

A CIP catalogue record for this book is available from the British Library.

ISBN 9781835694299

Printed in China

Discover more at
www.hungrytomato.com

Picture Credits
(abbreviations: t = top; b = bottom; m = middle; l = left; r = right; bg = background)

Wikipedia: By Tricia Robinson - http://landspeedevents.com/blog/ack-attack-worlds-fastest-motorcycle/, Fair use, https://en.wikipedia.org/w/index.php?curid=56819481 27b. Shutterstock: abdul hafiz ab hamid 17mr; Abdul Razak Latif 14-15bg, 15tr; ahmad.faizal 27tl; Anatoliy Lukich 11br; Anatoliy Lukich 20b; Antonio Guillem 5tr; Christian Bertrand 12m; Corinna Huter 26tl; Dave Hewison Photography 11m; Dziurek 21Ttr; Edu_2ev 5bl; Edu_2ev 5tl; Hafiz Johari 16-17b; Harman01828 5tr; Hazrin CRIC 4br; hurricanehank 28-29bg; Jan.Melichar 13ml, 13mr; JazzyGeo 25tr; Lario Tus 22-23bg; Mark_studio 18m; Mark_studio 4-5b; Michael Potts F1 26br; mooinblack 24bg; mooinblack 5tm; n_defender 9tl; OB production 8ml, 8br, 9bl; Oleksandr Lysenko 32b; Phil Jones 19m; Phillip Rubino 5br; Pushkarev Evgeniy 30-31b; Rainer Herhaus 17tr; Rodrigo Garrido 13bl; Ryan Fletcher 23tr; Sasha Zai 10m; Stefan Holm 21ml; Ted_Howells 7br; Toa55 9mr.

Every effort has been made to trace the copyright holders and we apologise in advance for any unintentional omissions. We would be pleased to insert the appropriate credit in any subsequent edition of this publication.